Disney Theatrical Productions
under the direction of
Thomas Schumacher
presents

Disney **Aladdin**
BROADWAY'S NEW MUSICAL COMEDY

Music by
ALAN MENKEN

Lyrics by
HOWARD ASHMAN
TIM RICE and **CHAD BEGUELIN**

Based on the Disney film written by RON CLEMENTS, JOHN MUSKER, TED ELLIOTT & TERRY ROSSIO and directed and produced by

Starring
ADAM JACOBS

JAMES MONROE IGLEHART   **COURTNEY REED**

BRIAN GONZALEZ   BRANDON O'NEILL   JONATHAN SCHWARTZ

CLIFTON DAVIS   DON DARRYL RIVERA

MERWIN FOARD   MICHAEL JAMES SCOTT

and

JONATHAN FREEMAN

as "Jafar"

TIA ALTINAY MIKE CANNON ANDREW CAO LAURYN CIARDULLO JOSHUA DELA CRUZ
YUREL ECHEZARRETA DAISY HOBBS DONALD JONES, JR. ADAM KAOKEPT NIKKI LONG STANLEY MARTIN
BRANDT MARTINEZ MICHAEL MINDLIN RHEA PATTERSON BOBBY PESTKA KHORI MICHELLE PETINAUD
ARIEL REID JENNIFER RIAS TRENT SAUNDERS JAZ SEALEY DENNIS STOWE MARISHA WALLACE BUD WEBER

Associate Producer
ANNE QUART

Technical Supervision
GEOFFREY QUART/
HUDSON THEATRICAL ASSOCIATES

Production Supervisor
CLIFFORD SCHWARTZ

General Managers
MYRIAH BASH
EDUARDO CASTRO

Associate Director
SCOTT TAYLOR

Associate Choreographer
JOHN MacINNIS

Casting
TARA RUBIN CASTING
ERIC WOODALL, CSA

Dance Music Arrangements
GLEN KELLY

Music Coordinator
HOWARD JOINES

Fight Direction
J. ALLEN SUDDETH

Production Stage Manager
JIMMIE LEE SMITH

Sound Design
KEN TRAVIS

Hair Design
JOSH MARQUETTE

Makeup Design
MILAGROS MEDINA-CERDEIRA

Illusion Design
JIM STEINMEYER

Costume Design
GREGG BARNES

Lighting Design
NATASHA KATZ

Scenic Design
BOB CROWLEY

Orchestrations
DANNY TROOB

Music Supervision
Incidental Music & Vocal Arrangements
MICHAEL KOSARIN

Directed and Choreographed by
CASEY NICHOLAW

The premiere of *Aladdin* was produced by The 5th Avenue Theatre in Seattle, WA. David Armstrong, Executive Producer & Artistic Director;
Bernadine C. Griffin, Managing Director; Bill Berry, Producing Director.

Cover Artwork © Disney
Production photos by Deen van Meer
Additional photos by Matthew Murphy and Cylla von Tiedemann

ISBN 978-1-4803-8679-2

Walt Disney Music Company
Wonderland Music Company, Inc.

DISTRIBUTED BY

HAL•LEONARD®
CORPORATION

7777 W. BLUEMOUND RD. P.O. BOX 13819 MILWAUKEE, WI 53213

In Australia Contact:
Hal Leonard Australia Pty. Ltd.
4 Lentara Court
Cheltenham, Victoria, 3192 Australia
Email: ausadmin@halleonard.com.au

Visit Hal Leonard Online at
www.halleonard.com

JAMES MONROE IGLEHART

Arabian Nights

DON DARRYL RIVERA, JONATHAN FREEMAN

ADAM JACOBS, COURTNEY REED

ADAM JACOBS

ADAM JACOBS, COURTNEY REED

ARABIAN NIGHTS

Lyrics by HOWARD ASHMAN
Music by ALAN MENKEN

Misterioso ♩ = 128

GENIE: Oh, I come from a land, from a far-a-way place where the car-a-van cam-els roam. Where it's flat and im-mense and the

ONE JUMP AHEAD

Music by ALAN MENKEN
Lyrics by TIM RICE

One hit a-head of the flock. ___ I think I'll

take a stroll a-round the block.

ENSEMBLE:

Stop, thief! ___ Van - dal! ___ Out - rage! ___ Scan - dal. ___

ALADDIN:

Let's not be too has - ty. _____

ADAM JACOBS

ONE JUMP AHEAD
(Reprise)

Music by ALAN MENKEN
Lyrics by TIM RICE

PROUD OF YOUR BOY

Music by ALAN MENKEN
Lyrics by HOWARD ASHMAN

THESE PALACE WALLS

Music by ALAN MENKEN
Lyrics by CHAD BEGUELIN

BABKAK, OMAR, ALADDIN, KASSIM

Lyrics by HOWARD ASHMAN
Music by ALAN MENKEN

JAMES MONROE IGLEHART

A MILLION MILES AWAY

Music by ALAN MENKEN
Lyrics by CHAD BEGUELIN

DON DARRYL RIVERA, JONATHAN FREEMAN

DIAMOND IN THE ROUGH

Music by ALAN MENKEN
Lyrics by CHAD BEGUELIN

Sinister, rubato

JAFAR:
You have the pro-file of a

Quick Tango (♩ = 134)

prince, with a phy-sique that match - es.

Be - neath the dirt and patch - es, you are a dia-mond in the

FRIEND LIKE ME

Music by ALAN MENKEN
Lyrics by HOWARD ASHMAN

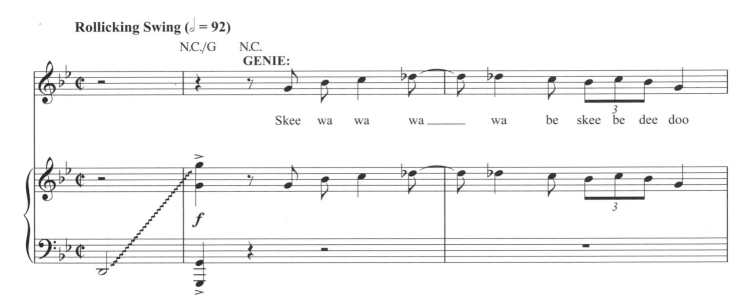

GENIE:
Skee wa wa wa___ wa be skee be dee doo

ba da da ba wa wap wa___ wa ba skee be da wap wap wa de a dah wah___

ALADDIN:
___ Can you give me a ba di ya da da da, ba di ya da da da,

PRINCE ALI

Lyrics by HOWARD ASHMAN
Music by ALAN MENKEN

1930's Jazz, Swing 8ths (♩ = 90)

90

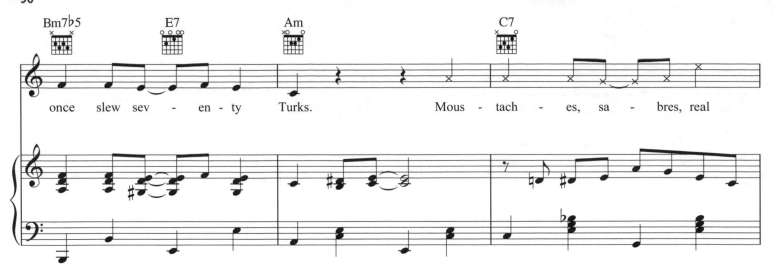

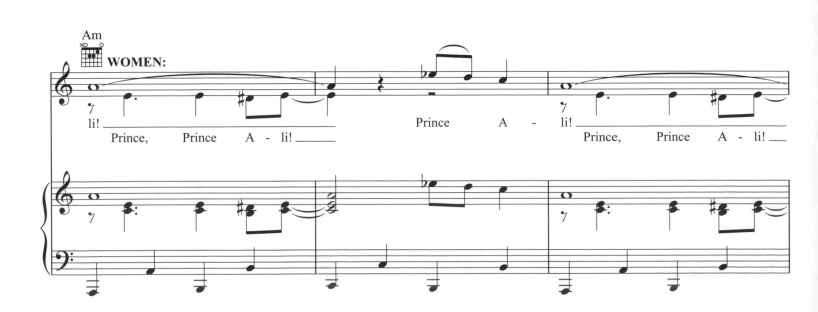

A WHOLE NEW WORLD

Music by ALAN MENKEN
Lyrics by TIM RICE

113

HIGH ADVENTURE

Lyrics by HOWARD ASHMAN
Music by ALAN MENKEN

BABKAK: Con- vince those guys, my lord and mas - ter.

Well, do it fast - er, let's be

SOMEBODY'S GOT YOUR BACK

Music by ALAN MENKEN
Lyrics by CHAD BEGUELIN

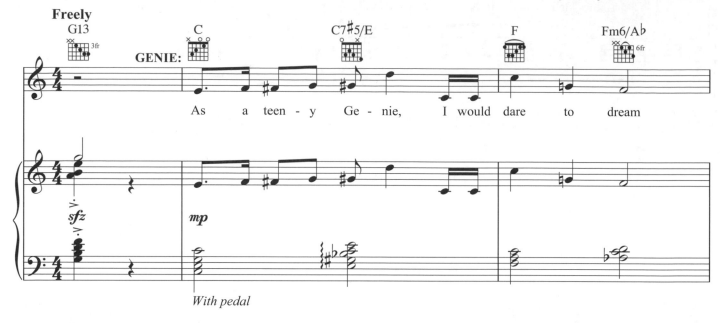

GENIE:
As a teen-y Ge-nie, I would dare to dream

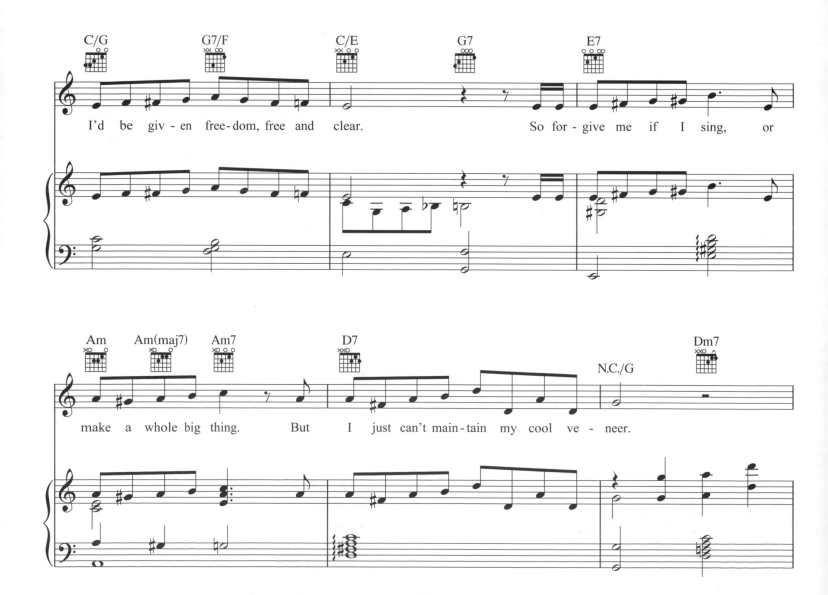

I'd be giv-en free-dom, free and clear. So for-give me if I sing, or

make a whole big thing. But I just can't main-tain my cool ve-neer.

COURTNEY REED, ADAM JACOBS